LIFE/DEATH

LIFE/DEATH

MARTIN SKIPTON

MARBLEIGH

Contents

The Raven's Call	1
The Flower and the Tree	4
The Letter	7
Voicenote	10
The Tale of Flame and Shadow	12
To the Me I haven't Met Yet	18
Farewell Glass	20
The View of an Angel	22
Life in a Day	25
Kaela's Last Kiss	27
The Maze	34
How Grief Feels for Me	37
The Final Leaf	40
The Tree in Me	42
The Long Drive	45
Season of Grief	48

The Day After	50
First and Last	52
The Echo	54
The Tale of Eryndor	56
Garden Reborn	60
The Conversation	62
Truce	65
Life Begins Again	67
The Shadow	69
The Little Things	72
What the Wind Remembers	74
The Day the World Stopped	77
Letter From Death	79
The Backwards Road	81
The Mountain of Days	85
The Poet and the Shadow	87
The Moment Between	90
The Gardener	92
One More Yesterday	95
The River	97
The Tide	99
How Will I Be Remembered?	101
Life	103
The Prince and the Rose	105

~ *VII*

Dance of Life	110
A Thank You to Life	112
The Failed Race	114
Life Unborn	116
One More Day	118
The Tapestry	121
When Life Loved Death	124
Heart and Mind	127
The Colour of Grief	130
The Trial of Death in the Court of the Gods	133
The Steps Towards	139
Letter to You	141
The Rose	144
Goodbye	146
Last Farewell	148
Lovers in the First Light	150

Copyright © 2025 by Martin Skipton, Marleigh Publishing House
All rights reserved. No part of this book may be reproduced in any manner whatsoever without written permission except in the case of brief quotations embodied in critical articles and reviews.
First Printing, 2025

The Raven's Call

Beneath the moon's pale soft light,
Where ivy chokes the tombstones white,
I lie in stillness, frail and old,
A breath away from being cold.

The chamber reeks of Laudanum dreams,
As time leaks out in silver streams.
The drapes are drawn, the clock is stopped.
All sounds but one have slowly dropped.

For at my sill, with eyes of coal,
A raven croaks to claim my soul.
Its wings are dusk, its voice is knell,
It sings of crypt and Asphodel.

It waits, unmoved by plea or prayer,

A sentinel in the cold still air.
Its gaze unblinking, meaning clear.
The hour has come, I must draw near.

I once was proud, a man of name,
With fortune vast and gilded frame.
But what are crowns or velvet beds,
When fever burns and reason shreds?

The lamp is low, the coals grow cold,
My hand no longer grasps the gold.
And yet I feel no fear at all.
There's comfort in the raven's call.

"Come," it whispers, "come away,
Where graves are soft and skies are grey.
Your sins are sewn, your debts are done,
Your dusk begins, but mine's begun."

I cough, I bleed, I scarcely see,
As shadows slip inside of me.
The priest has gone, the nurse has fled.
They fear to speak among the dead.

But still the raven keeps his post,
My single guest, my final host.
He bows his head and folds each wing,
A priest to ease my suffering.

Now breath is brief, and bones are chill,
And silence reigns, both stern and still.
Yet I go not in pain nor thrall.
I rise to meet the raven's call.

The Flower and the Tree

Flower:
Hello, old one. Your bark is cracked,
And moss sleeps where leaves once sang.
Does it hurt, to bend so low,
To stand so still beneath the sky?

Tree:
Little bloom, you are soft with spring,
Your petals still taste of dew.
No, it doesn't hurt to bow.
It hurts more to forget the wind.

Flower:
You remember the wind?
I've only just met her.
She danced past me this morning,

And I laughed until I shook.

Tree:
I remember her in all her moods.
She was wild once.
Tore through me in youth,
left my limbs tangled in stars.
Now she just hums lullabies
And combs my leaves like hair.

Flower:
What is it like, to be tall?
To see the birds before they land?

Tree:
Lonely, at times.
But worth it.
To shelter nests in your ribs,
To feel the sun not as warmth,
But as a promise.

Flower:
And when the cold comes?
When the bees forget your name?

Tree:
You let go.
Of leaves, of time, of need.

And still, something grows.
Not from you,
But because of you.

Flower:
Will that be me?

Tree:
Yes.
And one day,
You'll speak to something smaller still.
A seed, a whisper.
A green hope in the dark.

Flower:
When I meet them,
I will tell them,
You were not just falling.
Never falling.
You were making space.

Tree:
Thank you, little one.
I go then, with a smile.
And with hope.
Knowing you'll be here once I'm gone.

The Letter

Dear Mother,
The dusk is quiet now. A prayer without a name.
The wind has folded all the flags and killed the crackling flame.
I meant to write to you sooner, but the stars came down too fast,
and time here drips like candle wax that never seems to last.

Tell Anna I still wear her locket on my chest.
Her face is safe inside it, where my heartbeat finds its rest.
The fields are not like home here, Mother, though the grass is just as green.
The dead and damned lie beneath it, where our footprints should have been.

The captain said we'd travel back before the frost would bite,

But snow is here now and it doesn't care who's wrong or right.

Each step I take, I hold the names of those who have fallen to the deep.

And though I walk alone now, I am too afraid to sleep.

I'll keep marching on and let my heartbeat keep my pace,

Praying that each step takes me further from this place.

There'll be no rest for me, Mother, not while the guns still ring.

None will rest at all, not while war has a song to sing.

If I am late, it'll be because I'm slowed down by my fears.

Don't fill your heart with sorrow, Mother, don't waste your time with tears.

Bury not my memory, let it bloom just like spring flowers.

For what we leave in silence, may haunt the darkest hours.

And should they say I vanished, or was lost without a trace,

Know I became the soil, part of this accursed place.

I do not write to haunt you, Mother, but to hold you in the light.

I'll be the breath before the dawn, the light before the night.

So keep the kettle singing, let the curtains softly close.

I'll be coming home in poppies, Mother, draped in the colour of the rose.

Voicenote

Hey...
I know you can't hit "play" on this,
But maybe somewhere past the mist,
You're listening, or just nearby.
A whisper folded in the sky.

I thought by now I'd find the words,
But silence hums the loudest hurts.
Some days I speak with no one to care.
But still, I talk, pretend you're there.

The world keeps moving, cruel and kind.
Still I keep you inside my mind.
Like pages worn from being read,
Or songs we played before the dread.

Your laugh still echoes down the hall,
I replay all the words I still recall.
And sometimes when the night is long,
I swear I hear you in a song.

I miss the things I didn't say.
And the fights, the jokes, the lazy days.
I'd trade the moon to call your name
and hear you answer just the same.

Anyway...
I hope it's peaceful where you are.
No pain, no fear, just light and stars.
If love can reach beyond regret,
Then know, I haven't forgotten you yet.

Talk soon,
Or maybe just... listen.

The Tale of Flame and Shadow

I. The First Flame

In the silence before the world began,
When time was but a whispered plan,
There stirred a spark, a seed of light.
The primal flame that pierced the night.
It breathed, it sang, it danced alone,
And from its heart the world was grown.

The oceans drank its molten cry,
The mountains heaved beneath the sky.

Stars awoke with song from silent stone.
A choir of flame and flesh and bone.
From this first breath, the earth was crowned,
And life rose trembling from the ground.

The forest stretched, the rivers rolled,
The winds were young, the sun was bold.
Beasts were born from dream and clay,
And humans woke to shape the day.
They learned to speak, to fight, to feel,
To curse the gods and pray for meal.

II. The Shadow Walks

But where the flame did bright unfold,
A shadow stirred in caverns cold.
No voice it had, no breath, no face,
Yet moved it did through time and space.
Its name was Death, a thought unmade,
A silence sharp as unsheathed blade.

It watched the stars begin to die.
It felt the heartbeat's final sigh.
It walked behind each living creature,
A patient king and silent teacher.
It knew not hate, it bore no scorn.
Its gift was peace to those forlorn.

And so it came, as must all ends,
To shepherd kings and forgotten friends.
It whispered soft to old and young,
Its song a hymn not yet unsung.
Though feared, it came with gentle hand.
A ferryman to an unknown land.

III. The War Within

But humankind, with burning soul,
Resisted fate, defied the toll.
They built with stone, with fire, with steel.
A world of thought, a world to feel.
Yet every joy, each fleeting breath,
Still echoed near the steps of Death.

And so they waged a war of time,
With every birth, with every rhyme.
They wrote of gods, of stars, of strife.
To stretch the bounds of fragile life.
Their art was fire, their love a flame,
That Death could never quite reclaim.

For even as the last light waned,
And weary hearts no strength retained.
A child was born, a song begun,

A phoenix rising with the sun.
And thus the dance would start anew,
Where flame and shadow ever flew.

IV. The Reckoning

Then came an age of atom bending.
Of towers tall and wars unending.
The world grew wise, yet lost its way.
A night that wore the mask of day.
And Death walked swift, a roaring tide.
As life cried out, but none replied.

Yet in the ash, one seed remained,
A whisper where the world was pained.
A mother sang, a candle burned,
A child wept, and hope returned.
For though the shadow dark and deep,
The fire of heart did never sleep.

V. The Circle Turns

And now we stand, both flame and dust,
With eyes of wonder, bones of rust.
We live, we die, and in between,
We dream of things we've never seen.

And though the shadow walks behind,
Its presence shapes the soul refined.

For Death is not the end of all,
But part of life. The rise. The fall.
A gate through which all must descend.
Not a destroyer, but a friend.
For life. The spark. The fleeting breath,
Is made more precious by its death.

VI. The Final Song.

So sing, O stars, of light and doom,
Of flowers blooming over tomb.
For every end becomes a start,
And every grave can grow a heart.
This is the tale that has no end.
Of foe and flame, of death and friend.

We are the breath, the sword, the stone.
We walk this world, yet not alone.
In every life, the flame still lies,
Reflected in a thousand skies.
And when at last we sleep beneath,
May love be louder than our grief.

Thus ends the tale, both dark and bright,
Of death's soft shadow. Life's fierce light.

To the Me I haven't Met Yet

I hope you've learned to walk more slow.
To let the small winds guide your flow.
Not every fire needs be stoked to flame.
Not every loss requires a name.

I hope you've made your peace with change,
With seasons shifting, rearranged.
That you've stopped gripping things too tight,
And sleep untroubled through the night.

I hope you've loved with open hands,
And built your life on shifting sands.

Not fearing what might wash away,
But dancing in the break of day.

I hope regret no longer clings.
That time has softened sharper things.
That you've learned the gift of letting be.
I hope you look back, proud of me.

I hope you still find joy in rain,
In swirling water and windowpanes.
That laughter still feels close and loud,
And solitude is not a cloud.

And most of all, I hope you see
That who you are has set you free.
That all the paths and turns and strife
Have gently shaped a kinder life.

So if you read this, worn and wise,
With softer heart and steady eyes,
Know this… I tried to build the ground
You're standing on with the love I've found.

Farewell Glass

Do not mourn for me,
Just raise a farewell glass.
Wipe your tears.
Dry your eyes.
This pain will come to pass.

I travelled every road,
Drank deep from every hour.
Remember that,
When you think of me.
There's no need to feel so sour.

I never just passed through,
I left footprints in the flame.
But now I'm gone,
And it's ok

If life never feels the same.

So raise your farewell glass,
And picture me with mine.
Drink a toast,
Then get on with life.
It's your turn now to shine.

The View of an Angel

*I*t is quiet here.
Not silent,
   but a kind of stillness that cradles the soul.
   Like hands cupped around a cup of hot chocolate.

I have no heartbeat now,
Yet I remember the way mine once raced,
When I ran through fields,
Without a reason
Except to feel the wind rush to calm me.

Up here, time doesn't pass.
It hovers,
Like light before the dawn
That sees the sun cresting the horizon.
But memory,

Memory burns bright.

I remember the weight of grief
And how it taught me tenderness.
I remember holding someone's hand
Just because they needed it.

I miss.
The sound of rain against the roof.
The creak of an old chair.
The warmth of bread,
fresh from the oven.

Nothing eternal smells like cinnamon.
Only Earth gave me that.

I lived quietly.
No monuments bear my name.
But I loved.
I forgave.
I learned how to let go,
And then how to hold on again.

Now I watch.
I guide.
I send silence like a prayer,
To those still stumbling toward the light.

But sometimes,
Just sometimes,
I wish I could feel grass
beneath my feet
One more time.

Life in a Day

I was born at dawn in a cradle of gold,
Where the sky stretched wide and the air was cold.
The light was soft, and the world was new,
And everything shimmered in morning dew.

By breakfast, I learned to laugh and cry,
To point at clouds drifting lazy and high.
My hands were small, my wonder vast,
The moment slow, but growing fast.

By mid-morning I had learned to run,
To chase the wind, to greet the sun.
The hours danced, and I along,
To the rhythm of life's beating song.

At noon I stood in finest form,
A body strong, a spirit warm.
I built and dreamed, I spoke with fire,
My gaze ambition and desire.

Then afternoon, where edges dim,
A moment paused, a softened hymn.
I loved, I lost, I made amends.
I watched fresh faces change to friends.

By evening light, I slowed my pace,
Lines of time upon my face.
The world grew quiet, full of grace,
And I began to leave no trace.

At dusk, I sighed a final breath,
The day knelt down and welcomed death.
But oh what colour filled the sky!
Not an end, but a soft goodbye.

So if you ask how long life stays,
I'll say it fits inside one day.
From breath to breath, from sun to shade.
A life begins, is lived, then fades.

Kaela's Last Kiss

I. The Oath in Ash

In lands where stars like cinders fall
And ravens speak the ancient call,
There lived a blade-born warrior queen,
Named Kaela of the forest green.
Her name was sung in twilight's tongue,
Where wars were waged and heroes hung.

But love had carved a deeper hurt
Than sword or flame in fields of dirt.
Her heart belonged to one long dead.
A poet slain with blood-filled red.
He fell to fate's unkind design.
His soul dragged past the mortal line.

By night she knelt beside his grave,
And swore beneath the wind and wave,
"If gods will not return his breath,
Then I shall breach the gates of Death.
Not for spite, nor longer life,
But just one last kiss, 'tween man and wife."

II. The First Descent

She sought the crone beneath the hill,
Who brewed her tea with fire and pill.
"Seven levels," the old one hissed,
"Through wrath and fire, storm and mist.
But know this well, my darling dove...
Hell does not suffer acts of love."

With steel in hand and sorrow drawn,
She pierced the veil before the dawn.
The earth gave way to blood-red light,
And swallowed her in choking night.

III. The Circle of Flame

The first of Hell was scorched and wide,
Where sins ignited on the tide.
Here tyrants screamed in endless burn.
And devils danced at every turn.

But Kaela walked through blistered fire.
Her breath a blade, her bones desire.
A demon rose with coal-black wings.
It sneered and hissed infernal things.

"Why trade your flesh for fleeting breath?
Why court the kiss of burning death?"
She answered not with words, but flame,
And called the dark one's immortal name.

IV. The Lake of Lies

Next came a place where truth unspoke.
Where mirrors wept and promise broke.
False voices echoed from the deep.
Her lover's tone, his endless weep.

But Kaela knew that Hell deceives,
That memory wears masks like leaves.
She slashed through phantoms, voice and fear.

Till silence caught the dark lord's ear.

V. The Howling Dark

The third was made of wind and roar,
Of sinners lost in blood and gore.
Here wandered those who preyed on kin,
Now blind with guilt, and bound within.

Kaela, strong, yet shaken still,
Felt every scream like sharpened chill.
A thousand hands reached up from dust,
But could not move her iron trust.

VI. The Garden of Ash

Then came a glade of twisted bloom.
Where dark flowers fed on doom and gloom.
The trees all whispered, sweet and sly,
"Rest sweet Kaela. Let your quest die."

She pressed on, though roots did bind.
She fought them back with will and mind.
No thorn could halt her final vow,

No petaled trick could stall her now.

VII. The Throne of Teeth

At last she reached the blackest throne.
Where sin itself had turned to bone.
The ruler there was vast and thin.
A mouth of void. A grinless grin.

"I know you, warrior. Know your pain.
But none will take from my domain."
She said, "I have not come to steal,
But simply kiss what once was real."

The figure laughed, then moved aside.
There he stood. Pale. Wide-eyed.
Her poet love, in shadows dressed.
With no more blood to warm his chest.

VIII. The Kiss

She cupped his face, her calloused palm
A moonlight touch in realms of harm.
She kissed him once. No more, no less.

A trembling, bittersweet caress.

And in that kiss, he breathed again,
If just for heartbeats counted ten.
He wept a tear of molten stone,
And whispered, "Now I am not alone."

IX. Return

Then Death himself, who watched them both,
Let fall his blade, and broke his oath.
"To love," he said, "I bow but once.
Now go you must, for darkness hunts."

She turned alone. She could not stay.
But on her lips still burned that day.
She rose from Hell, her soul alight,
With fire forged in love and fight.

X. The Song of Kaela

So sing of her with triumphant breath,
Who walked the stairways down through Death.
Not for glory, pride, or fame.

But just to speak her lover's name.

And in the stars, some still believe,
A kiss can light all those who grieve.
And Kaela's tale will never fade.
For love like that cannot be unmade.

The Maze

Life is a maze of shifting walls.
Of endless paths and sudden falls.
We step inside with hearts unsure.
Each turn a test we must endure.

The start is bright, the laughter near.
With voices warm and futures clear.
We chase the light, we chase the sound.
Until the first dead end is found.

We wonder while we can't go on,
What other walls we'll come upon.
Why can't we just walk straight and true
Why must the end remain from view?

Some doors swing wide, then close with grace.

Some lead us back to the same old place.
We lose our way, we lose our will.
We stand in silence, soft and still.

Love greets us down a hidden lane.
A fleeting kiss, a touch, a name.
But love can drift, or choose to stay.
And either road can lead astray.

Loss waits behind a shadowed wall.
A sudden stop, a crushing call.
It carves a space where joy once grew,
And leaves us changed, and searching too.

Yet in the dark, we learn to feel.
We learn our strength, we learn to heal.
We find the courage to walk the maze,
To walk, to fight, to dim the blaze.

The twists remain, the trials stay.
But still we move, we make our way.
Until at last, breathless and scared,
We reach the centre waiting there.

Not made of gold or grand parade,
But peace within the life we made.
The maze was never meant to trap.
But guide us through each thunderclap.

For every turn that felt unfair
Was part of how we made it there.
And in the centre, calm and true,
We find ourselves, reborn, and new.

How Grief Feels for Me

Grief doesn't knock,
It just moves in.
Takes the spare room
And paints the walls
A colour I don't recognise.

It eats at strange hours,
Sleeps in late,
leaves the lights on
And the washing up not done.
And I let it.
Because I don't know how to ask it to leave.

Grief doesn't wail, not always.
Sometimes, it whispers.
In the shower.

In the dark.
In the quiet part of a song
I used to love.

It feels like forgetting what laughter feels like,
But remembering every word you said.
It's reaching for my phone
To tell you something
And realizing
I can't.

It's the way sunlight looks wrong now.
Too soft.
Too sharp.
Like the world kept going
And I can't.

Grief is private.
People ask how I am,
And I say "I'm okay,"
Because it's easier
Than saying
"My chest is full of broken glass
And I'm trying not to move too much."

It comes in waves,
But no one told me...
Sometimes the tide pulls back

So quietly until
I think it's over.
And then it hits again.
Hard.

I carry it.
Not with strength,
But with surrender.
I stopped trying to fight it.
Now I let it walk beside me.
Not in front.
Not behind.
Just… with me.

That's how grief feels for me.
It changed me.
Not all at once.
Not for worse or for better.
Just permanently.
Permanently.

The Final Leaf

Alone it clings, the dying flame.
A trembling leaf without a name.
While all its kin have flown and gone,
It greets the dusk, the cold, the dawn.

Its veins are drawn in amber thread,
A memory once green, now red.
Into the hush of autumn's breath,
Between the breach of life and death.

The branches croon their creaking song.
The nights grow sharp, the days grow long.
But still it waits. Not out of fear.
It holds a tale for one to hear.

A gust arrives with curious grace,

And curls around the leaf's still face.
It bends, it leans, it almost breaks.
Then to the wind its tale it makes:

"I saw the spring, the buds unfold.
The bees, the light, the rain, the gold.
I danced with light, I drank the sky.
Now let me go, it's my time to die."

The wind, in silence, takes the gift,
And with a breath, begins to lift
The leaf away, with solemn care
A final whisper through the air.

The Tree in Me

I am the branch, but not alone.
I bloom from roots I've never known.
Each ring of bark, each weathered scar,
Tells me how I've come so far.

I am my father's measured tone,
The way he made the world his own.
His steady hands, his guarded smile,
That held his storms with quiet style.

I am my granddad's stubborn fire,
His grit that climbed through muck and mire.
He walked through life with love and pride,
And never let the world decide.

I am my grandma's gentle hand,

The calm that helped me understand.
She spoke in deeds, not loud acclaim,
And lit our home with just my name.

I am my great-grandmother's grace,
The way she lit a shadowed place.
With gentle strength and knowing eyes,
She sowed her peace where sorrow lies.

Their lives live on in voice and stance,
In how I weep, and laugh, and dance.
A woven thread, both strong and true,
I am the old, yet something new.

And now my children bloom in me.
New shoots upon this family tree.
They carry sparks from all I've known,
And roots they'll one day call their own.

They'll take my voice, my flaws, my name,
My whispered dreams, my quiet flame.
And mix them with their own bright fire,
To build a life, to climb up higher.

For every branch must bend and grow,
And reach for light we may not know.
But still we pass from seed to leaf,
Our love, our loss, our joy, our grief.

So here I stand, not first, not last.
A living echo of the past.
And in my arms, the yet-to-be.
The future fruit upon this tree.

The Long Drive

Life is a road trip, strange and wide,
With no set map, just stars to guide.
The engine hums with hope and fear.
Who's behind the wheel? Not clear.

At times, I swear it's firmly me,
Hands gripped tight, wild-hearted and free.
I set the course, I choose the song,
But blink, and someone moves in strong.

A parent drove the early miles,
With warnings, snacks, and knowing smiles.
We passed through towns with names I miss,
Like 'Innocence' and 'First-time Kiss.'

Later, friends would take the wheel,
With reckless turns and spinning zeal.
We laughed through nights that blurred the line
Between the foolish and divine.

Lovers drove with fingers laced,
Through winding roads and open space.
Some exits hurt, some caused delay.
Some promises just slowly frayed.

I've passed the places I've called home.
Left pieces on the way I've roamed.
Regrets are signs you sometimes keep,
They flicker by, but don't run deep.

Now solo, mostly, as I steer,
The rearview holds both loss and cheer.
Ahead, the road is veiled and vast.
No telling how long the drive will last.

But somewhere near the far-off bend,
I hope it slows, not meets an end.
A cabin lit, a gentle hill,
A place where all is warm and still.

Till then I drive, the sky unrolled,
Through thunderstorms and light struck gold.

With miles to go, and songs to play,
And faith that I'll be okay someday.

Season of Grief

Grief is the winter that nobody chose.
Arriving in silence on ground that froze.
It drapes the sky in a heavier grey,
And steals the songs that once knew how to stay.

The trees wear loss like tattered lace.
Bare-limbed shadows in empty space.
The wind is a whisper you almost hear.
A name, a laugh, nothing dear.

It tastes like smoke and unshed tears.
A slow-cooked ache that waits for years.
Time walks slower through fields gone bare,
And memory blooms in the coldest air.

Yet under the frost, the roots still cling,

Dreaming quietly of some distant spring.
Grief does not pass, it shifts its shape,
Like light through ice, or breath through drape.

You learn to walk on frozen ground.
To plant small joys where none are found.
And though the thaw feels far away,
Even winter begins to fray.

Then one bright morning, soft and brief,
You'll find the green beneath the grief.

The Day After

The sun rose like it always does,
  Though nothing feels the same.
Its light spills soft on silent walls,
But cannot speak your name.
You left us behind so suddenly,
It's as tough you were never here.
A trace of breath, a worn-out chair,
a laugh I strain to hear.

The kettle boils, the cups laid out.
I pour two like before.
I set one down, then take it back,
Forgetting you're no more.
The house is thick with quiet now.
Too loud to let me rest.
Your shoes still by the doorway lie,

As if you'd just gone west.

The clock insists on ticking on,
A cruel relentless thing.
The world spins on its axis still,
While mine has lost its ring.
I walk the rooms like haunted halls,
Your absence fills the air.
My fingers trailing memories.
as if they'd still be there.

The phone stays mute, the bed half-made.
A shrine to all you were.
Your scent still clings to fabric folds.
A ghost that doesn't stir.
And though the grief has yet to bloom
It builds inside my chest.
Today, I simply sit and breathe
And try my very best.

Oh life that dares to carry on.
Oh love that couldn't stay.
Oh how the sky can still be blue
On this first, empty day.

First and Last

The First Breath:
The world begins in sudden light,
A tremble in the womb of night.
A gasp, a cry, the silence torn.
From empty hush, a soul is born.

Fists unfurl like waking stars,
Lungs fill with air from realms afar.
The skin meets sky, the pulse takes flame.
Breath becomes the voice of name.

The Last Breath:
The world recedes to dimming light,
An evanesce to end the flight.
A sigh, a pause, the tether breaks.

From restless hours, a soul unmakes.

Hands fall still like cooling stars,
Lungs send the air to where dreams are.
The skin forgets, the pulse grows mild.
And peace returns to what once was wild.

The Echo

*T*hey will not carve their name in stone,
Nor raise a glass tower alone.
No anthem follows where they went.
No monument, no grand event.

But still they're there, in morning light.
In how you pause before the night.
In folded cloth, in garden rows.
In quiet ways that kindness grows.

They're in the laugh you didn't know
Was borrowed from them long ago.
The steady calm you found one day
Was once their hand that led the way.

Their voice remains in a certain songs,

In knowing what to do when wrongs
have torn the world or bruised your pride.
You hear them walking by your side.

Not legacy in gilded frame,
But in the way you speak their name.
In silence deep where grief once sat,
They linger soft, and more than that...

They change the shape of how you see
The smallest things: a cup of tea,
A well-worn book, the evening air,
They leave their soul still everywhere.

No fame, no wealth, no worldly claim,
Just echoes warm, without a name.
And what remains when they are gone
Is love, passed gently, on and on.

The Tale of Eryndor

In lands where shadows kissed the ground,
And time ran soft without a sound,
There dwelled a knight of heart and flame,
Eryndor was his valiant name.

He'd conquered storms, defied the gods.
Split oceans wide with iron rods.
No foe had brought him to his knee.
No beast, no man, no tyranny.

But whispers stirred the midnight air,
Of one last foe who did not care
For swords or shields or mortal fame.
For Death had come, and spoke his name.

Eryndor blinked and blinked again,
From immortal foe he could not restrain
His warrior's passion or need to win.
He readied himself for battle's begin.

It came not cloaked in gloom or spite,
But veiled in stillness, pale and white.
With eyes like stars long burned away.
And footsteps soft as breaking day.

"I come," it said, "as all things end.
Not as a foe, but as a friend."
Eryndor laughed, his blade held high,
"You'll not take me while I can try."

He struck with fire, he swung with wrath,
He carved through air and split the path.
But Death just watched with quiet grace,
A calm expression on its face.

For every blow that Eryndor dealt,
No wound appeared, no pain was felt.
The fields grew old, the flowers died.
The world itself seemed to subside.

Days passed, or years. It's hard to say.
For time and thought both slipped away.

Still Eryndor stood, proud and worn,
His armour rusted, blade now torn.

And Death then spoke in solemn tone,
"You fight, yet still you walk alone.
But know this truth, before you fall...
To live is not to win at all.

You've loved, you've wept, you've sung your song.
And now you've lingered far too long.
The end is not a thief or curse,
But rest well-earned, for best or worse."

The knight sank down upon one knee,
His eyes no longer seeking spree.
He saw his past in fleeting light,
A child's laugh, a lover's flight.

And there he wept, not out of fear,
But for the grace that drew so near.
He dropped his sword, then bowed his head,
And whispered, "Take me home," he said.

So Death reached out with open hand,
And led him to a quieter land.
Not void, nor dark, but full and wide,
Where all who lived and loved reside.

And thus the tale of Eryndor ends.
Not slain, but met by one who mends.
For death, he found, is not defeat,
But where the soul and silence meet.

Garden Reborn

The wind still moves the silent trees,
 Though now they bend with softer grace.
The sun still warms the morning leaves,
Though shadows linger in their place.

The laughter once that filled the air,
Now echoes in the quiet light.
A voice that's gone, yet everywhere,
In dreams, in dusk, in stars at night.

Grief is not a closing door,
But steps that lead through weeping rain,
To find, beneath the hurt we bore,
New roots of love, still touched by pain.

For though one heart has ceased its beat,

The world does not forget its song.
The birds still give their notes so sweet.
The rivers find their path along.

We carry you in breath and bone.
In folded clothes, in cups of tea.
In moments when we feel alone,
You're there in silent memory.

And life goes on, not quite the same,
But rich with all you left behind.
A flame still dancing in the rain,
A gentle voice within the mind.

So let the seasons turn again.
Let petals fall and new ones grow.
Love doesn't die, it just remains
In quieter ways than first we know.

The Conversation

I found you where the dreamer lives.
Beneath the elm, the windless sky.
No breath, no weight, and yet you spoke
As if you'd only paused to die.

"Sit down," you said, "it's quiet here.
The world won't miss you for a while.
Tell me of days you cherish most.
I'll tell you of the golden isle."

You looked the same, yet not at all.
Your eyes like light behind a veil.
I asked if death had brought you peace.
You gave a slow and sombre exhale.

"Peace? Just distance. Clearer sight.

Things I thought would make me whole?
They vanished when I left the flesh.
Love mattered more than any goal."

"Regret?" I asked. You turned away.
The sky hung dull as you replied,
"I chased the clocks, I missed the stars.
I waited years to truly say...

'I love you', not in passing tone,
But like a vow before the flame.
Too proud, too lost, too full of plans,
And thinking time would stay the same."

My heart beat fast, my head spun quick.
Your voice was wind and rising tide.
"So tell them now," you whispered low.
"Don't wait for death to be your guide.

I never thought that time would end,
I never paid it any due.
That's the regret I leave behind,
What I would have done different, If I knew

Live not as if the end is far.
But as a fire that's burning fast.
Hold hands too long, forgive too soon.
And protect your truth as though it's glass."

The light had changed. You had to go.
Your shape a ripple in the air.
"Remember this," you said and smiled,
"The dead don't need your grief. Just care."

Truce

How dare you leave without goodbye!
No warning note, no lullaby.
You slipped into that silent night,
While I was screaming for the light.

I cursed your name beneath my breath,
Furious at your quiet death.
You promised me you'd always stay!
What made you want to go away?

I raged at stars, at sky, at sun,
At every morning that would come.
How dare the world keep spinning still,
When mine had shattered and left me chill?

Your laughter haunts the empty hall.
It mocks the quiet of it all.
And every corner holds your trace.
Your scent, your voice, your sacred place.

But time, the thief, began to mend.
Each wound it carved, it dared to tend.
And in the dark, I found a spark...
Your love, still glowing in the dark.

I saw you in the autumn trees,
In whispered winds and dancing leaves.
In songs you sang and books you read.
In dreams that kissed my weary head.

You didn't leave me, not for good.
You stayed in all the ways you could.
Not bound by breath or fragile bone
But sewn in memory all my own.

So here's my truce, my final cry...
I'll let you go. But not goodbye.
We'll meet on the road again someday,
I'll never again let you go away.

Life Begins Again

The chair is still, the room is bare.
Yet traces linger in the air.
A scent, a laugh, a half-spoken line.
A moment frozen out of time.

The world did not come to a close,
When your hands stilled, when your eyes froze.
But something paused, a breath held tight.
A shadow cast in morning light.

And still, outside, the robins sing.
The roses bloom, the church bells ring.
The kettle boils, the floorboards creak,
And days go on, though hearts feel weak.

Grief walks beside, a quiet friend.

Its weight may shift, but doesn't end.
Yet in its embrace, life finds a place.
A tender bloom in loss's grace.

We laugh again, though not the same.
And speak aloud your precious name.
In tears, in joy, we learn to bear
The love that lingers everywhere.

A sunrise breaks the longest night.
A child runs chasing morning light.
The seasons turn, the stars remain,
And so, with time, life begins again.

The Shadow

Grief is a shadow that trails behind.
A silent shape that clings and binds.
At first, it loomed like night's own chill,
Heavy, dark, and stubborn still.

It draped itself across my days.
A cloak of sorrow, thick with haze.
Each step I took was slow and small.
Beneath that weight, I feared to fall.

The world was bright, but through that veil,
Colours dulled and faces pale.
I walked a path both cold and thin,
With grief as night, and me within.

That shadow stretched, immense and wide.
A mountain pressing by my side.
It whispered doubts, it stole my will.
A voice that urged me not to heal.

But time, the slow and steady friend,
Began to mould and shape its end.
The shadow softened, lost its edge.
No longer chained to every pledge.

It shrank to just a pale outline,
Less a chain and more a sign.
A trace of what I've had to lose,
A quiet part I cannot refuse.

Though still it walks beside my feet,
Its heaviness now less complete.
It bends and flows, light as air.
A presence gentle, almost fair.

The shadow taught me how to feel.
Grief, though sharp, can also heal.
It marked the love that once was here,
A silent love that's still sincere.

So now I walk with lighter pace.
The shadow softens in its place.

Not gone, but changed, a softer chill.
  A part of me, forever still.

The Little Things

I fold the clothes and sweep the floor.
The kettle hums its tune once more.
I water plants you used to tend.
I catch myself then just pretend.

Your coat still hangs behind the door,
Your slippers rest upon the floor.
I dust around them, soft and slow,
As if you might come back and know.

I pay the bills, I check the post.
I mend a button, cook a roast.
The dog still waits beside your chair,
He looks, then cries, cause you're not there.

The world is held in tasks so small.

A list, a load, a daily call.
And in their rhythm, I survive.
One breath, one chore, still half-alive.

I cook the meals you used to crave,
I tend the flowers on your grave.
The quiet grows, but still I move.
In every act, I find a groove.

For grief is not just tears and ache,
It's bread to slice, a bed to make.
It's sweeping crumbs you'll never see.
A thousand things that carry me.

And though you're gone, I carry through,
Each little task, a thread of you.
Until these hands, through time and grace,
Make peace within your empty space.

What the Wind Remembers

I was born when world was whispering flame,
 Before your kind gave storms a name.
I blew through halls of mountain stones,
Long before you claimed divided thrones.

I've danced through forests and castle walls.
 Heard lullabies and battle calls.
I've cooled the brows of kings and slaves,
And scattered dust on unmarked graves.

I've stolen breath and stoked your fires,
I've stirred the heat of bold desires.

I've circled brides in veils of lace,
Then moaned across her lover's face.

You do not see me, yet I trace
Each line of grief upon your face.
I hold the echoes of your cries
When you say your final goodbyes.

I watched you build with trembling hands,
Raise spires high on shifting sands.
Then watched you tear it down again.
Out of hunger, fear, division or pain.

I've brushed the pages of your books,
Heard secrets shared in shadowed nooks.
I've swept through wars, both just and blind.
And cried with songs you left behind.

I've heard your children laugh and scream,
Felt joy like fire, and loss like steam.
I've known the weight of final breath.
The silence that follows after death.

But still you rise, you write, you bleed.
You sing of love. You plant a seed.
You bury dead with trembling hand
And still make music across the land.

What do I feel, you wonder now?
I've no heart, no soul, no furrowed brow.
But if I could, I'd weep and soar
For how you love despite the roar.

I envy not your mortal years,
But how you hold them close with tears.
You live, you break, you burn, you bend,
And still you rise and rise again.

So when you hear me through the trees,
Know this...I carry memories.
Of every birth, and breath, and tomb.
I bear your joy. I bear your gloom.

And when you're gone, I'll still be there,
A hush, a gust, a ghost of air.
I'll hum your names beneath the stars,
And sing of all the things you are.

The Day the World Stopped

The sun forgot to rise that morn,
Its golden fingers broken, torn.
The sky and clouds refused to break,
A quiet voice whispered "Hold, don't wake."

The clock's hands hung in frozen place,
No ticking in the empty space.
The birds fell static in mid-flight.
Even the wind lost all its bite.

The trees stood rigid with leaves like stone,
Roots clutching earth, but stood alone.

The river paused, a halted flow,
Its waters quiet, dark, and slow.

The air grew thick as shadows spread,
A weight that pressed on every thread.
The world became a fragile thing,
Each heartbeat slow, a muted ring.

Inside the chest where laughter grew,
Now hollow echoes whispered through
A void where light once softly played.
A garden stripped, its blossoms flayed.

For in that moment, time had bled,
And something precious somewhere had fled.
The earth kept turning, yet it stopped,
The day the heart inside me dropped.

That day the world forgot to spin,
Held hostage by the loss within.
And though the sun would rise again,
It never quite expelled the pain.

Letter From Death

Dear Ones,

I write not with a scythe in hand,
But with a feather, soft and worn.
No darker than a dusk-filled sky,
No crueller than the day you're born.

You paint me shadow, name me fear,
Yet I do not devour.
I close the eyes too tired to see.
And the body's final hour.

I do not steal, I only keep
What time has asked you to release.
I do not rush, I always wait

Until your soul begins to cease.

You call me cold, but I have knelt
At every bed where pain does burn.
You've cursed my name, yet I have wept
For all the ones who won't return.

But know this truth, I will not change.
I am the shore, the easing tide.
The place you come to lay the weight,
Of what your flesh has pushed aside.

I hold no malice, make no claim.
I only do what must be done.
And if I come with quiet steps,
It's not to shadow the setting sun.

So live your days with open hands,
And when you see me, do not run.
For I will come like dusk to stars,
Not snuffing a light, but showing one.

Yours always,
—Death

The Backwards Road

I. The Ending That Begins

He woke beneath an ancient sky,
Skin like parchment, breath a sigh.
The world was slow, a softened hum.
Wasting beneath a setting sun.
But something stirred behind his eyes,
Not fading light, but young sunrise.
He stood not bent, but growing tall.
Unravelling his final fall.

His name was Edward. Time's mistake.
A man the world forgot to break.

Born as helpless as any babe,
And yet a breath length from the grave.
With silver hair and wrinkled hands,
He had not life, but shifting sands.
And yet each step he took unmade
The brittle shell that time had laid.

II. The Dance of Years Unwinding

Each morning younger than the last.
He shed the silence of the past.
His back grew strong, his vision clear.
His voice rang full from ear to ear.
Memories fell like golden leaves,
But backward. Dreams he once believed.
Like lovers he had thought once lost,
Were still await with their cost.

He learned to walk, then learned to run,
And marvelled at the morning sun.
A widower's grief, once heavy chain,
Uncoiled into a lover's name.
He kissed her in the rain one night,
Then met her eyes in sweet delight.
And finally, in trembling bliss,
He asked her name before the kiss.

III. The World Grows Wide Again

The wars he fought became a game,
The medals vanished, so did shame.
His hands let go of tools and steel,
And found again what youth can feel.
He danced through halls of sleepless years,
Until the world forgot its tears.
He laughed and sang his heart's delight,
No thought given to the coming night.

He shrank into a laughing boy,
Barefoot in a field of joy.
No past to chase, no wounds to hide,
Just grass-stained knees and reckless pride.
The sky grew tall, the stars more bright,
His dreams not memories, but flight.
He learned the names of all around,
Taking joy in all he found.

IV. The Silence Before Sound

He learned to speak, then learned to hum,
And soon forgot where songs came from.

Words dissolved, then thoughts, then name.
A crib became his final frame.
His mother's arms, the softest gate,
Held him as he shed all weight.

His eyes grew wide, then slowly closed,
The world a soundless bloom of rose.
Not death, this time, but something new,
A doorway to a whole new view.

V. And So...

The backward road he walked alone
Was not a curse, nor weighted stone.
For every soul is born to die,
But few get time to ask it why.
And he, who travelled life reverse,
Saw every blessing in the curse.

He learned what most may never see...
The end begins where we are free.

The Mountain of Days

Life is a mountain I strive to climb,
One jagged edge, one hand at a time.
Each morning greets me cold and steep,
With dreams to chase and wounds to keep.

I hoist the pack of yesterdays,
A weight I've borne through shifting haze.
Some stones are loss, some forged in fear,
Yet still I pull them year to year.

The sun may shine, then fade to grey,
And fog may steal the light away.
But still I climb, though bruised and slow,
Through winds that howl and frozen snow.

At times I stumble, ache, and crawl,

The summit high, the ledge too small.
But even when my footing slips,
I grip the rock with finger tips.

For every scar has shaped my tread,
Each sorrow taught. Each time I bled.
And those I've met along the trail,
Their voices rise when mine would fail.

The climb is long, the air turns thin,
Yet still I feel the fire within.
For whispers speak of skies so wide,
Where stars and silence gently bide.

And when I reach that final crest,
With heaving heart inside my chest,
I'll turn and see where I began,
Each valley crossed, each path I ran.

The view will stretch like painted grace,
With all I've faced etched in its face.
And I will smile, no need to speak,
For every climb was worth the peak.

The Poet and the Shadow

In lands where dawn and twilight blend,
There lived a poet, a cherished friend.
With pen in hand and heart afire,
He ran from fear that would not tire.

A shadow followed, cold and fleet,
A silent step behind his beat.
Not friend, not foe, but ever near,
The whisper none would name or hear.

From youth he sought to outrun fate,
To cage the dark that stalked his gait.
With ink and verse, with rhyme and prose,
He trapped the ghost in fragile pose.

He wrote of death, a cruel, grim guest,
   A spectre that would never rest.
Each line a chain, each stanza snare,
   A hope to hold it prisoner there.

He penned of graves beneath the moon,
   Of fleeting life, and ending soon.
His words were swords, his verses shields,
   In battles fought on endless fields.

Yet still the shadow would not cease,
   It lingered close, denied release.
It shaped his nights and stole his days,
   And haunted in a thousand ways.

Through mountains high and valleys low,
   The poet wandered, voice aglow.
He sought the secrets none could find,
   The key to flee the dark behind.

But years wore thin, and flesh grew frail,
   And even words began to pale.
His final scroll, his last refrain?
A song that welcomed relief from pain.

Then on a dusk as amber bed,
The shadow touched his weary head.

No scream, no fight, no final breath,
  The poet met his twin in Death.

  And in that moment, face to face,
No fear remained, no time, no place.
Two equals bowed with calm respect,
A truth their souls could now reflect.

 For death, he learned, is not the thief,
  But guardian of life's brief motif.
   And poetry, that fleeting spark,
    Gave fire to the coming dark.

  So hand in hand they walked away,
    Into the folds of endless grey.
  The poet's voice, a gentle thread,
Still weaves the tale though he is dead.

The Moment Between

*T*here's a silence the world has never heard.
A silence shaped like breath undone.
Where light forgets which way to fall
And time no longer needs to run.

My body floats beneath me now.
A hollow boat on memory's tide.
Each heartbeat echoes softer still.
A tide that ebbs with no moon to guide.

I feel the pull of something vast.
Not cruel, nor kind. Just true, just there.
A velvet dark that holds no fear,
And something bright beyond the air.

The voices near me fade to mist.

Like names in dreams I can't recall.
And every pain unthreads itself,
Each tether slips without a fall.

One moment more, then none at all.
A breath half-taken, not released.
And in that pause I understand
That what we are is never ceased.

Not light, not dust, not even thought.
But something still, and wide, and deep.
I do not fall. I do not rise.
I only drift into the sleep.

The Gardener

The field of life in sunrise rest,
  Petal, flower, crawling pest.
 Each falling leaf will play its part,
 As long as the Gardener has a heart.

 He walks the rows with silent tread,
 A hooded figure, black in thread.
 Of night and wind, with hands that tear.
 Yet gentle in the morning air.

 He does not wield a scythe or flame,
 But answers only to one name.
 His spade is time, his shears are fate.
 He prunes the early, and the late.

 Each soul a seed, each life a stem,

He tends them not for gold or gem,
But leans to whisper, soft and low,
And helps the quiet roots to grow.

He waters grief and joy alike,
Where roses bloom and thistles strike.
He knows which blossoms must be trimmed.
When petals fold, when light has dimmed.

Some vines he winds with sweet repose,
Some thorns he trims to save the rose.
He plants with care and not with haste,
No bloom, to him, is ever waste.

A wilted leaf, a fallen bloom,
He lays them down with no assume
Of cruelty or of cold disdain.
Just compost rich from love and pain.

He does not grieve the fading leaf,
For in decay, he sees belief
That life will root again in spring.
A cycle spun on endless ring.

And when he turns to you one day,
He will not speak, but guide the way
Through garden paths you once called strife,
To where the soil births new life.

So fear him not, this keeper true,
Who tends to me as he tends to you.
For death's no end, nor cruel thief
But gardener of all living grief.

One More Yesterday

I lie beneath this fading light,
Where shadows stretch into the night.
The ticking clock, a mournful bell.
That tolls the end I know too well.

Oh, if I could just steal away.
One fragile breath, one more yesterday.
To feel the sun upon my face.
To hold again that lost embrace.

The laughter from a distant past.
A moment bright, too sweet to last.
A whispered word, a gentle touch.
I crave these things, I miss them much.

But time is cruel, it will not stay.

It pulls me from my yesterday.
And though my heart may plead and ache,
I cannot bend the steps I take.

So here I rest, with eyes half-closed.
Dreaming a life I've not disclosed.
One last glance before the night.
One more yesterday, one last...

The River

Life is a river, winding and wide.
Born from the mountains where dreams reside.
It dances through valleys, it crashes through stone.
Carving a path that is wholly its own.

At first, it's a stream with a curious pace.
Skipping through childhood with innocent grace.
It gathers the rains of joy and of fears,
Growing in strength through the flowing of years.

It bends around loss, it swells with desire,
It cools in the shade, it burns like a fire.
Sometimes it stills where the heart feels alone.
Sometimes it rages with a will of it's own.

It carries the driftwood of sorrow and loss.

The faces we've loved, the places we cross.
Some moments go under, some memories stay.
All flowing onward, then drifting away.

We try to steer, to chart and command,
But often it slips through the grip of our hand.
Yet somehow it teaches, with each rise and each fall,
That letting it carry us leads through it all.

And when it slows near the end of the line,
It carries our hearts, both yours and mine.
A river not ending, but joining the sea.
A life ever flowing, boundless and free.

The Tide

Life rolls like waves upon the shore.
Sometimes it lifts us, sometimes more.
It pulls us down into the deep,
Then carries us on heights to keep.

The sun will rise, then clouds will fall.
We stumble hard, yet still stand tall.
With every loss, a lesson learned.
With every scar, a victory earned.

The laughter rings, then silence drums.
The heart will break, the spirit hums.
A dance of shadows, light, and rain.
A blend of pleasure mixed with pain.

Failures come like sudden storms,

Yet through them grows a thousand forms.
Of strength, resolve, and clearer sight,
That shape us in our darkest night.

Triumphs bloom like flowers wild.
Unexpected, sweet and mild.
Moments when the world aligns,
And all the stars begin to shine.

So hold the lows, embrace the highs.
The stormy seas, the open skies.
For in the ebb and in the flow,
We learn, we grow, we come to know,

That life's a journey, ever spun.
Of battles lost and battles won.
A story told in highs and lows.
The beauty in the tide that flows.

How Will I Be Remembered?

I feel the weight of fading time,
A whispered end, a final rhyme.
Before the dark, I pause and fear,
Will anyone remember me here?

In stories told or silence deep,
Will echoes of my soul still keep?
A spark of light, a gentle hand,
Or shadows cast upon the land?

Was I friend or caused regret?
Was kindness given or neglect?
Do hearts recall a smile I gave,
Or pain I left before the grave?

I wonder how my name will live?
In love, or wounds I did not forgive?
And if I fade without a sound,
Will peace or blame be all around?

Still, here I stand,
Both proud and small,
Hoping, just hoping
That I matter after all.

Life

Life is a spark on a canvas wide,
A flicker of light we're asked to ride.
A breath, a blink, a rising sun.
A race begun when none have won.

It's laughter spilled on kitchen floors,
A half-shy kiss behind closed doors.
The smell of rain on thirsty stone.
The hush of night when you're alone.

It's music played with trembling hand.
The strength to hope, the will to stand.
A baby's cry, a final sigh.
The questions asked, the reasons why.

It's morning tea, warm and sweet.

The stranger's smile you chance to meet.
A story told with wrinkled grace.
The soft remembering of a face.

It's falling down and rising strong.
The pull to sing your one true song.
To love, to lose, to try once more.
To knock, unsure, on life's wide door.

No map is drawn, no lines are straight.
Yet still we walk, we dream, we wait.
And every step, both joy and strife,
Is woven in the cloth of life.

The Prince and the Rose

I. The Shadow Comes

In lands where silver rivers run,
Beneath the gaze of moon and sun,
A kingdom shadowed by mountain steep,
Where kings were crowned and dragons sleep.
Prince Anton, born of starlit flame,
Was heir to valour, sword, and name.
A youth not yet to winters ten,
But bold as far more seasoned men.
Yet death came swift on silent wing,
One night beneath the whispering spring.
A fever deep, a trembling hand.
The reaper stalked across the land.

II. The Realm Between

In half-lit halls of spectral mist,
Where memories and time desist,
Young Anton walked with breath grown thin,
Past veils that part the world within.
He found a throne of bone and ash,
Where Death, in robe of midnight sash,
Sat still as stone with hollow gaze,
Unmoved by pleas or mortal praise.
Yet in the prince's hand there shone
A bloom unknown to any one.
A single rose, blood-red and bright,
Its petals kissed by dawn's own light.

III. The Prince's Plea

"Keeper of the final door,
I beg thee, wait a moment more.
I've not yet fought, nor led, nor kissed.
It is not my time, I must resist!
My sword is sharp, my heart is wild,
Yet still I am a mother's child.

Take not this youth before its rise,
And I shall give my dearest prize."
He held the rose with trembling care,
　Its fragrance soft upon the air.
　"A gift for you, O Death so cold.
A rose that never shall grow old.
It blooms with hope that will not die.
　It weeps for stars in every sky.
　It is the love I've yet to give,
If you but simply let me live."

IV. Death Replies

The silence stretched, a crushing tide,
As Death in shadowed voice replied
　"I've taken kings, and knelt to none.
　My path is set, my task begun.
No flower, bright though may be,
　Can halt the pull of destiny."
　But then he gazed upon the rose.
It did not wilt, nor bend, nor close.
Its petals burned with crimson grace,
　As if it knew no time nor place.
"What magic binds this bloom so still?"
Death asked, voice like winter's chill.

"No magic, sir," the boy replied,
"Just all the love I hold inside."

V. The Bargain

And Death was still. The silence spoke
Of shattered chains and burdens broke.
For once, the scythe hand dropped in rest.
No blood, no scream, no sins confessed.
"I've taken much, but never known
A gift not born of fear alone.
You offer me not bribe nor plea,
But beauty given willingly."
He stood and let the darkness part,
Then touched the rose upon his heart.
"You live, young prince, and rise anew.
But know one day I'll come for you."

VI. The Return

Then Anton woke in morning's gleam,
As if returning from a dream.
His fever broke, his breath restored,
As sunlight spilled across the floor.

He rose, a child with eyes now old,
Who'd bargained with the dusk and cold.
He bore no scar, save one unseen,
A coldness from whence he'd been.
And in his garden, tall and proud,
Where flowers bloomed in scented cloud,
One rose stood bright, untouched by years.
A tale of hope, of love, of tears.

VII. The Echo

So sing, O bards, with voice like flame,
Of Anton's rose and Death's own name.
How life, though fleeting, dares to stay
When love stands firm to bar the way.
Let every child who fears the night
Take comfort in that rose's light.
For all now know what Anton knows,
Even Death paused for a single rose.

Dance of Life

Life is a dance, a whispered sway.
A step we learn along the way.
Someone will lead, with steady grace,
Another will follow, finding their place.

The floor is wide, the lights are dim.
The song begins with hopeful whim.
At times, a waltz, so slow, refined,
Then quickstep beats that leave us blind.

Hands clasp, then part, then clasp again.
Some partners leave, some still remain.
A glance, a turn, a borrowed breath.
Each twirl defies the pull of death.

The music shifts, we shift as well,

To moody blues or brass's swell.
And though our steps may sometimes stray.
The rhythm calls, we find our way.

No dance repeats, no song the same.
Yet all who move still play the game.
With grace or stumbles, we advance,
This fleeting, pulsing, sacred dance.

A Thank You to Life

Oh life, I raise my voice to you,
For all the pain you've put me through.
The nights I wept, the days I soared,
The silent wounds, the strength restored.

You gave me light, then showed me dark.
You lit the flame, then dimmed the spark.
In every loss, a seed was sown,
A deeper truth I've come to own.

You burned my soul with grief and fire,
Then crowned the ash with new desire.
You let me stumble, break, and bend,
Then placed a sunrise at the end.

You dressed the world in joy and ache,

In every storm, a chance to wake.
You showed me triumph isn't clean,
It's messy, raw, and sometimes mean.

But oh, how sweet the breath I take,
When dreams arise for hope's own sake.
The broken glass beneath my feet,
Still led me here to something sweet.

So thank you, life, for all your ways.
For shadowed nights and golden days.
For love that left, and love that stayed,
For every choice that I have made.

No perfect path, no painless climb,
Yet all of it, a gift in time.
You gave me tears and let me grow.
A beauty born from ebb and flow.

The Failed Race

He ran beneath the shifting sun,
A race that never could be won.
Each step away from silent breath,
A desperate dash from looming death.

He counted seconds, dodged the night,
Avoided shadows, feared the light.
Plans were drawn with fragile lines,
To keep the clock from its designs.

He built his walls with wary hands,
To hold the time, to bar the sands.
But in his fortress, cold and bare,
He found no time for tender care.

Years slipped by like fleeting smoke,
And promises he never spoke.
Moments passed but never seized.
Life's soft song forever teased.

Then came a quiet evening's sigh,
When he stopped and dared to try,
To look around, to breathe, to see,
What lay beyond mortality.

And in that stillness, clear and wide,
He met the truth he'd long denied...
In fearing death, he'd lost the art,
Of living fully, heart to heart.

No battle won against the tide.
No victory in running wide.
For life is not a place to hide,
But a journey lived, not just survived.

Life Unborn

You stir beneath my heartbeat's flutter,
  A quiet ripple, soft and new.
  I speak to you through woven skin,
  Though you don't yet know the sound of who.

The world is vast and stitched with fire,
With oceans deep and skies unkind.
But, my child, there's also light.
When love and heart are strong combined

You'll taste both laughter and the rain.
The kind that chills, the kind that soothes.
You'll learn that love is not a chain,
But a wind that lifts, and hands that move.

You may be broken, once or twice.

This world can bend a soul.
But even broken things can sing.
You'll find your voice, and make it whole.

Some days will come with hollow hours,
Where silence knocks and fear is loud.
But hope, my love, is stubborn too.
It defeats the dark, it parts the cloud.

I cannot shield you from the ache,
From loss, from time, from bitter truth.
But I can give you all I have.
My arms, my name, my quiet truth.

That you were dreamed before the stars,
And carried long before the light.
That even in this trembling love,
You are my courage, not my fright.

So grow, my child, and greet the sun.
Not with fear, but open hands.
This life is yours, both sharp and sweet.
I'll walk beside, while I still can.

One More Day

In silence deep, where shadows lie,
Stuck beneath a hollow sky.
No stars to mark the midnight true,
No light to guide a heart that's blue.

A voice within begins to wane.
Soft murmurs shaped from grief and pain.
The walls close in, the air grows thin.
A war of thoughts begins within.

"I'm tired," they whisper to the night,
"Of climbing walls that have no height.
Each smile I wear is stitched with pain.
Each step I take washed out by rain."

Memories flicker. A dim-lit reel

Of laughter faded, wounds that heal
Too slow, too shallow, not enough.
The path ahead too steep, too rough.

The moonlight glints. The blade, a gleam.
A final end. A quiet dream.
A thought, so tempting, cold, and wide
To leave the ache of life behind.

They hold it gently in the light,
One quick flick to stop the night,
To stop the heartache, stop the pain,
And never feel this way again.

But as the edge comes into view,
A fragile voice comes breaking through.
Not loud, not brave, but a trembling cry.
"Just stay," it says. "Don't say goodbye."

"One more breath. One more try.
Before you tell the world goodbye.
Just one more throw until you know,
You don't have to face this life alone."

And so they sit, in the dark of night,
And see something just in sight.
A thread of hope, so faint, so frayed.
But enough, perhaps, for one more day.

So on they walk, through night's long shade,
With quiet courage. A little less afraid.
No promise made, no grand display.
Just strength enough for one more day.

The Tapestry

Upon the loom where time is strung,
Where threads of breath are softly spun,
Life weaves its tale in ice and blaze.
A tapestry of fleeting days.

The image starts with slender white.
The thread of birth, of dawn's first light.
So fine, so pale, it barely shows,
Yet holds the weight of all that grows.

Then begin the colours bold,
Crimson cries and hopes untold.
First laughter loops in hoops of gold.
A mother's hand, a story old.

Soft blue threads of childhood skies

Are knotted through with wide-eyed tries.
Skinned knees, deep dreams, the endless run
Beneath the heat of summer sun.

Then storms arrive in charcoal thread,
The tangled thoughts that twist the head.
The knots of doubt of aching loss,
Are woven tight, each one a cross.

But here an emerald flame of choice,
A sudden turn, a lover's voice.
A pattern flares, the loom grows fast,
As fate and fire meet at last.

The reds of rage, the whites of peace,
The violet hours that never cease.
Each thread pulled taut in quiet grace,
Each fray repaired in its own place.

In time, the hands grow still and slow,
The colours dim, the stitches show.
Yet from afar, what once seemed flawed
Forms sacred shapes that leave you awed.

A spiral bloom from grief and grit,
A diamond spark in shadow lit.
A border sewn from all you gave,
Both what you lost and what you saved.

And when it ends, this woven sprawl,
It will not hang in silent hall.
It moves, it breathes. Each thread, each hue.
A mirror deep of all that's true.

So weave, though winds may shift the pain.,
Though threads may snap or warp with strain.
For every strand you place today
Becomes the shape of your display.

When Life Loved Death

*I*n the hush before the world began,
When stars were seeds and time a plan,
 Two forces stirred in cosmic breath,
 One called Life, the other Death.

Life rose up with a golden sun,
With songs of joy and endless fun.
She danced through stars, gave hearts their beat,
And scattered green beneath her feet.

Death was shadow, still and deep.
He whispered rest, he sang of sleep.
He moved with grace, in silence spun,
The night that balanced that fiery sun.

And when they met, the world held still,

As if the heavens bent to their will.
For in her eyes, he saw the spark
That soothed the ache within his dark.

And in his gaze, she saw the peace
That made her wild hunger cease.
They loved a love no rule could bind,
So fierce, so vast, so undefined.

But love, though true, was never free,
Not when twined with destiny.
For if they touched, if lips had met,
The balance broke, the end was set.

If Life embraced her solemn twin,
Then none would die, nor none begin.
And if Death held her far too tight,
Then nothing born would hold the light.

So gods wept hard and stars withdrew,
To see a love that could not do
What simpler hearts might dare to try.
To kiss, to stay, to live, to die.

Instead they danced the edge of fate,
Where dawn and dusk together wait.
She'd bloom a field, then step away.
He'd fold it gently into grey.

And though they pass but never meet,
They leave a trail of bittersweet.
In every birth, a hint of grief.
In every loss, love's trembling leaf.

They write the world in paradox.
A key that fits a thousand locks.
And so they move in rhythm deep.
She gives the breath, he grants the sleep.

No vows, no hands, no wedding bed,
Yet closer than the words we've said.
For Life and Death are lovers true,
Forever split, yet always two.

And if you pause between your days,
In quiet woods or starlit haze,
You just might feel them passing by,
One in your breath, one in your sigh.

Heart and Mind

Mind:
What is life but measured days?
A ticking clock, a plan well laid?
Purpose lies in order, thought,
In knowing how and why and aught.

Heart:
But what of songs that break the rules?
Of dancing lost in summer pools?
Meaning lives in warmth, not schemes!
It's found in fire, in tears, in dreams.

Mind:
Dreams are fragile, flickering things.
They fall apart when morning rings.
We need reason, solid ground!

Not hope that floats, not joy unbound.

Heart:
Yet without joy, what use is ground?
A path unloved is just a sound
Of footsteps echoing alone.
Even logic needs a home.

Mind:
Home is built from careful bricks.
Plans and paths, not hunches, tricks.
Feeling is fine, but not the guide.
We need a compass, not the tide.

Heart:
But I am the compass when you stray.
I feel the truth you think away.
Love has mapped more roads than fear!
And not all answers must be clear.

Mind:
Still, storms will come. We must prepare.
Feelings won't fix broken air.
Meaning needs a scaffolding.
Not just the bells, but what they ring.

Heart:
And I will ring them, every time.

With every ache, with every climb.
You build the world, we need your part.
But don't forget... I make it art!

Mind:
Perhaps you're right. We're halves, not whole.
You make it pulse. I shape the soul.

Heart:
Then walk with me. Through light, through strife.
Together, we'll give shape to life.

The Colour of Grief

Grief is not black.
No cloak, no veil, no midnight hue
Can hold the shape it folds into.
It's more the shade of storm-tossed skies.
A bruised and swollen compromise.
Between the dusk and coming rain.
The colour not of death, but pain.

It starts in blue, a breaking wave.
The quiet gasp you never gave.
A dusklight ink behind the eyes,
Where memories like gulls still rise.
It's teardrop blue, a cobalt flame,
That flickers soft around your name.

Then grief turns grey, a muted tone.

The ash of moments left alone.
The fog that creeps inside the chest,
Where time forgets how to progress.
It whispers dull through endless days.
In shadowed rooms and distant gaze.

It shifts to green, not life, but loss,
The moss that clings to weathered cross.
The emerald of a last goodbye,
That travels slow beneath the sky.
It is the mold on untouched bread.
The garden choked by words unsaid.

Then red, oh red, the sudden flare.
The howl beneath the silent prayer.
The ember rage that will not sleep.
The cut that makes the silence weep.
It strains the throat, it stains the bed.
It paints the dreams you wish were dead.

There's yellow too, but sickly pale.
The sunlight trapped in coffin nail.
The jaundiced joy you fake with grace.
The brittle mask upon your face.
A laugh too sharp, a smile too wide.
A colour you can't hold inside.

White comes last, not peace, not light,

But blankness thick as winter night.
The chalk where once a heart had bled.
A snow that falls where love has fled.
It's not an end, but more a pause.
A silence without sound or cause.

Grief is not black. It does not stay.
It changes shade from day to day.
A canvas stretched too tight, too wide.
Where every colour comes to hide.
And in its art, both cruel and true,
It paints the world in shades of you.

The Trial of Death in the Court of the Gods

In halls beyond the realm of time,
Where stars are not allowed to climb,
A court arose in heaven's dome,
Far from Hell and mortal home.

The pillars carved from cosmic dust,
The air was thick with ancient trust.
The judges sat on thrones of fire,
Old gods of storm, of sea, of lyre.

Zeus with lightning in his hand.
Odin with wisdom and power grand
Anubis dark with jackal's grin.

And Shiva, calm amidst the din.
Athena stood with sharpened spear,
While Thor rang Mjolnir loud and clear.

From east to west, from sky to shore,
The gods of myth returned once more.
Before them stood in cloak of black,
A figure dark, no soul to track.

His eyes were voids where silence sleeps.
His voice like wind through canyon deeps.
He bore no sword, no scythe or flame,
Yet all could feel his weight of name.
Death stood accused, now held to task.
Could purpose mask the price he asks?

Zeus struck his bolt upon the stone,
"O Death, who walks this world alone,
The cries of mortals flood the skies,
Explain thy path, thy truth, thy lies!
For every child, for every king,
You clip the thread, you snap the string.
Why must you steal the life from breath?
Defend thy cause, O Lord of Death!"

Death bowed his head with ghostly grace,
No fear upon his ageless face.
Then from the silence came his plea,

Words of solemn clarity.
"O mighty ones, I take no joy
In acts that grieve or lives destroy.
I am no villain, not by voice,
I act because I have no choice.
For life alone, unending, wide,
Becomes a cage, a curse, a tide.
Without my touch, there is no birth,
No meaning to your days on Earth.
Would poets write with hearts so deep
If none they loved were lost to sleep?
Would warriors fight with burning might
If all were spared from endless night?
Would lovers cling with passion's flame
If time did not erase their name?
The song of life requires its end,
And I, though feared, am but its friend."

Odin rose with single eye aglow:
"To end is fate, but must it show
So grim a face, so harsh a tone?
Could you not leave us peace, alone?"

"O All-Father," Death said with sigh,
"Even gods must one day die.
The tree you guard with raven's call
Knows every fruit in time must fall.
Your runes were carved in blood and pain,

And so is all that we sustain.
I do not come with hate or pride.
I am the ebb that follows tide."

Thor stepped forth with mighty pride,
"What of the warrior who has but tried,
To vanquish foes throughout the land?
You leave his bones upon the sand!
What my father says is true!
Why must all souls lie down to you?"
With that Thor did take repose,
And held aloft Mjolnir in a warrior's pose.

Athena stepped forth, brow held high,
"Yet how can wisdom justify
The theft of babes, the plague, the war?
Do you not leave the world a sore?"

"O Goddess born from heart divine,
Your realm and mine in shadows twine.
For every plague that I bestow,
A healer learns, a heart may grow.
For every sorrow death ignites,
A soul awakens, seeks new heights.
I am the dark that makes the day,
Without my hand, all light would stray."

Anubis, quiet as the sand,

Raised his scepter in his hand.
He spoke in tones of tomb and dust,
Of judgment weighed with ancient trust.
"I weigh the hearts, and I have seen
The peace your touch can grant between.
To mourn is hard, but in that pain
A truth is born, a pure domain.
Without your gate, there is no door,
No path to realms, no evermore."

Then Shiva stood, in still repose,
The dancer where creation flows.
He gazed at Death with knowing nod,
And whispered soft, "You are no fraud.
For I destroy, and yet I build.
Your silence leaves the soul fulfilled.
Let men lament, let mortals cry,
But none may live who will not die."

A hush fell over the sacred space.
Death bowed once more with timeless grace.
The gods conferred with voice and flame,
Their judgement called, their final claim.

Then Zeus arose, the skies grew bright,
His voice a storm, a bolt of light,
"We find no fault in Death today.
Let none defy his solemn way.

He is the dusk that gives the dawn,
The final breath when strength is gone.
Not curse, but part of nature's plan,
A shadow woven deep in man."

And so Death turned with softened pace,
No triumph writ upon his face.
He fades not out of spite or rage,
But closes life upon its page.

And as he passed from mythic throne,
He whispered soft, to gods alone:
"Remember me when stars descend,
For even Time must find its end."

Thus ends the tale, the trial grand,
Of Death who walks through every land.
No tyrant he, but keeper true,
Of life's last gift... the final view.

The Steps Towards

Each moment ticks, a step ahead.
A quiet path where all are led.
Toward the dusk, the final breath,
An inch by inch approach of death.

But if each step must take me there,
I'll walk with love and tender care.
Not hurried steps in blind regret,
But footprints one would not forget.

I'll greet the dawn, embrace the light.
Dance with the day, and hold the night.
Find meaning in the simple things.
The songs, the smiles that living brings.

For death's the end we all must face.

But life's the journey, not the race.
So every step, though closing in,
Is a chance to grow, to lose, to win.

And when my curtain call is done.
I'll stand up proud and know I've won.
For all my steps that they have seen
Will be there best there's ever been.

Letter to You

I still talk to you.
Not out loud, not always,
But in the quiet spaces.
When I pour my tea.
When I lie awake at night,
Staring at the ceiling
Because the world is wrong
Without you in it.

I want to say I'm okay.
That I'm healing.
That I've learned to smile again.
But the truth is...
Some days, breathing feels like betrayal.
Some days, I hate time
For moving forward

Like nothing happened.

You left,
And the world kept spinning.
How dare it?

I see things you would've loved,
A dumb joke,
A change in the weather,
The way the sky looks before a storm.
And I ache
Because I can't show you,
Can't hear you laugh,
Can't say, "look at this,"
And feel your eyes following mine.

I would give anything
For one more minute.
Not even a full day,
Just sixty seconds
To say
Everything
I didn't say.

I'm sorry if I ever made you feel
Unseen,
Unheard,
Unloved.

You were all of it to me.
Still are.

I don't know what happens after this.
If you're somewhere listening,
Or just gone,
And that thought terrifies me.
But I hope,
If there's even a sliver of you
Out there,
That you know this…

I miss you
With everything I have.
And I love you
With everything that's left.

Always.

The Rose

*I*n morning's warmth, the bud unfolds.
A whisper soft in sunlit gold.
   Its petals tight with dreams unseen,
   A cradle held in leaves of green.

   The dawn of life, so sweet, so shy.
   It lifts its head to touch the sky.
   Each drop of dew, a breath, a tear.
   Each moment born from love, not fear.

   The rose begins to open wide,
   With youthful fire and blushing pride.
   Its velvet bloom, both bold and bright,
   A testament to warmth and light.

   But time, the silent gardener, walks.

With patient hands removes dead stalks.
The sun now scorches, winds will bend.
Each joy must curve, each path descend.

The petals fade from red to rust,
Their silken edges kissed by dust.
The rose, once full, begins to bow.
But beauty lingers, even now.

Yet in the autumn, secretly sown,
In soil where shattered blooms are thrown,
A seed, unseen, begins to grow.
Into what we soon will know.

For life, like roses, folds and flows,
From birth to bloom to last repose.
And in decay, there waits a spark,
A bud preparing in the dark.

So mourn not what the rose has lost,
Each petal falls but pays no cost.
For every death, a breath anew.
And morning brings a brighter hue.

Goodbye

I stood beside your quiet bed,
The morning sun a muted red.
No more the rise, no more the fall.
Just stillness in the quiet hall.

Your hands, once warm with work and grace,
Lay folded now in perfect place.
I searched for words that might convey
The weight of what I could not say.

The clock ticked on. I held my breath,
Still trying to make some sense of death.
How terrible a thing that hearts can break
But still keep beating for god's sake.

I touched your cheek, so pale, so still,

And felt the love that time can't kill.
Your stories linger in the air,
Like whispered prayers and loving care.

You taught me how to tie my shoes,
To chase the wind, to win, to lose.
And now I learn, with tear-stained eyes,
The hardest lesson... how to rise.

I'll speak your name in quiet rooms,
In garden walks, in twilight blooms.
In every laugh and every tear.
I'll hold you close. You'll still be near.

So rest now, Mum, your journey's through.
I'll carry all I learned from you.
And when my own last breath is nigh,
I'll find you there.
For now.
Goodbye.

Last Farewell

I've danced with time, and time has led.
A gentle hand where I now tread.
This body's worn, a threadbare coat,
But oh, the tales it still can gloat.

The stars I've chased, the storms I've braved,
The hearts I've held, the tears I've saved.
And now I feel the evening's hush,
No fear, no fight, no frantic rush.

My bones creak tunes the young don't know.
Soft lullabies from long ago.
I've laughed till dawn, and wept at noon.
Held lovers close, then lost too soon.

I've known the sweet, I've tasted pain.

Each moment's been a worthy gain.
So let the final curtain fall.
I've heard the echo of life's last call.

No need for mourning, fret, or fuss.
Death's but a ride that waits for us.
I'll tip the driver, smile, and say,
"Thanks for the ride, now on my way."

And if you cry, then cry with grace.
But picture joy upon my face.
For I have lived, and I've lived well.
But for now, my friends, my last farewell.

Lovers in the First Light

I. Before the First Breath

In the dark before the birth of stars,
Where silence throbbed like ancient scars,
No fire burned, no shadows cast,
There dwelt two powers, First and Last.

Life, she danced on golden breeze.
A whisper through eternal seas.
With hands of flame and breath of bloom,
She sang of joy, and banished gloom.

Death, he lingered still and wide,
A presence deep as rolling tide.
With eyes of stone and obsidian heart,
He stilled the storm, and stopped the start.

Apart they stood, alone they reigned,
In realms where nothing yet was named.
She, the pulse. He, the cease.
She, the storm. He, the peace.

But one bright age, without a year,
Life turned, and Death drew near.
Not to conquer, not to claim,
But drawn by something none could name.

She touched his hand, a comet's kiss.
He sighed, and worlds began to hiss.
Within the void, where once was naught,
Their union sparked a primal thought.

No war, no clash of sword or scythe,
But aching love, Death danced with Life.
She bloomed with him as he faded in her,
And stars awoke with newborn stir.

They wove the cosmos, curve by curve,
Each heartbeat began the light and nerve.
And in that endless, shapeless night

She cried, a laugh, a moan, a light.

And from their kiss, so slow and wide,
A new thing stirred and turned inside.
A child, not born of blood nor breath,
But born of Life, and born of Death.

They named him Time, the eternal ring,
Who walks with paupers and with kings.
He never stops, he never stays,
He counts the dusk, he sows the days.

Time blinked and stars began to spin.
He wept and rain and tides begin.
He crawled and continents took their place.
He laughed and beasts began their race.

He ran and trees reached toward the sky.
He spoke and minds began to cry.
He dreamed and men with open eyes
Built towers tall and told him lies.

They watch as through the world he roams,
Life and Death, his heart, his home.
They birthed the song and keep the beat
Two lovers who no longer meet.

She gives, he takes. She builds, he breaks.

Yet both entwined in what they make.
And Time, their son, will always be
The thread of both. Eternity.

II. The March of Time

Time grew tall with breathless speed,
He learned to hunger, learned to need.
With every step, the cosmos changed.
What once was shapeless, now arranged.

He wandered through the morning mist
With fire-bright stars upon his wrist.
His footprints forged the endless stream
Where day and night began to dream.

He laid down seconds, stacked them high,
A ladder reaching through the sky.
From dusk to dawn, from seed to tree.
He named his rhythm Destiny.

Where once was void, now sang the spheres.
A clock was born from spinning years.
And from the cradle of his will,
The world awoke, both wild and still.

The Children of the Hour

Upon a plain of molten hue,
Time shaped the first of creatures true.
He whispered breath into their chest,
And Life stirred deep within their breast.

But always watching, still as sleep,
Death moved softly, slow and deep.
He did not strike, he did not shout,
He simply turned the soul lights out.

Thus, all things born began to fade.
From mountain stone to new-made blade.
From kingly beast to baby cry,
They bloomed, they broke, they learned to die.

Yet Life did not resist or mourn,
She kissed each soul as it was born.
Death watched from shadow life unfold,
And took each soul into his hold.

And Time, who watched them rise and fall,
Felt sorrow stir beneath it all.
He saw their dreams, their fleeting fight,

And wept for them each lonely night.

The Veil of Forgetting

In Time's great shadow, minds grew bright,
They lit their caves with stolen light.
They forged and fought, they lied and learned,
And still the stars above them burned.

They built up myths to veil the truth.
No memory of their maker's youth.
They sang of gods with flaming swords,
Of skies in war and thundering hordes.

Yet none recalled the first embrace,
The two who kissed in starless space.
The mother warm, the father still,
Who bore them Time with love and will.

But though forgotten, still they reign,
In every joy, in every pain.
When lovers part or children cry,
When old men kneel beneath the sky.

It is not gods whom they implore,
But Life who knocks, and Death at door.

And Time, who neither waits nor bends,
Moves on, though men do pretend.

III. The Fracturing of Time

Time, once flowing smooth and wide,
Began to twist, to crack, to slide.
For mortals, bold with baited breath,
Began to bargain Life and Death.

They forged tall towers made of thought,
Declared that Time could now be caught.
They carved him into gears and chimes,
Broke him into clocks and rhymes.

"Let hours bend beneath our hand!
Let future yield to what we've planned!"
They measured seconds, sold the years,
Chased away their primal fears.

And Time, once vast as ocean's swell,
Now found himself confined to bell,
To tick, to tock, to rigid rules.
A cage made by man's own tools.

The Tears of the Timeless

And Time began to ache and fray,
The brave new world led him astray.
He stumbled through the turning lands,
His veins now bound by mortal hands.

He saw them age, he saw them die,
He saw them curse the darkened sky.
He watched them hoard what could not last,
And beg for futures not yet passed.

He cried aloud: "I am your kin!
The thread you're in, the skin within!
I am the reason things unfold,
Not something you can count or hold!"

But none could hear his desperate moan,
For he had shaped them bone by bone.
And now they claimed him, root and stem,
And used his breath to bury them.

The Return of the First and the Last

Far off, in veils beyond the clock,
Where stars fall soft with silent shock,
Life stirred in her golden sleep
And whispered through the growing deep,

"My son is bleeding through the sky.
He limps, he falters, soon may die!
His joy is lost, his path unclear,
And still these creatures do not hear."

Then Death, who watched with solemn grace,
Took up his cloak and turned his face.
He spoke not much, but when he did,
The stars themselves in silence hid.

"Then let us go, just once again,
To walk among the sons of men.
For though they do not speak our name,
They burn with echoes of our flame."

The Hourglass Shatters

And so, as Time began to break,
His parents rose for mercy's sake.

They walked through ruins, fog, and steel,
Where nothing true was left to feel.

They found the cities drained of song,
The days felt short, the nights too long.
The mortals, aged by empty speed,
Still searched for more than they could need.

Then Life knelt low, and touched the ground,
And seeds rose up without a sound.
And Death, in turn, made shadows fall
To cradle silence over all.

And Time, their child, near broken, torn,
Felt once more how he'd been born.
Not to be mastered, chained or sold,
But witness to the brave and bold.

IV. The Remembrance of Fire

Time lay scattered, breathless, pale,
A winding thread, grown thin and frail.
The world still spun, but slow with grief,
Its stories shortened with dead belief.

The skies were grey. The oceans slept.

And even dreams no longer wept.
The mortal flame, once bold and bright,
Had dimmed beneath the weight of night.

But then came Life, with voice of flame,
Who called all creatures by their name.
She danced in fields of glass and stone,
And sang a song she'd once intoned.

A lullaby of breath and birth,
Of pain that carved the shape of worth.
And where she stepped, the flowers woke,
And dying hearts in silence spoke.

The Choice of The Child

Then Death, the quiet, kind, and cold,
Stood still as myths from ages old.
He touched no soul with sudden end,
But waited like a patient friend.

He whispered, not with threat or blade,
But asked if any were unafraid
To walk with him, to meet the dark,
To strike again the ancient spark.

And one rose up, a mortal child,
Her hands were worn, her eyes were wild.
She knelt beside the broken Time,
And said, "I'll give what still is mine.

I've lived, I've laughed, I've lost and learned,
Let now my ember be returned.
Let Time be whole, though I must part,
I give my breath, my blood, my heart."

The Rebirth of the Endless

Then Life wept once. Then Death did too.
Their tears were stars in morning dew.
Together, both with solemn grace,
They touched the child's upturned face.

The child gave her gift with heart,
And from solemn lands did depart.
Death held her hand and took her fear,
Life reached out and drew her near.

And Time, reborn in light and hush,
Awoke with dawn inside his blush.
He breathed again, and now he knew,
To end, to start, were both to do.

No longer bound by clock or chain,
He flowed like mist, like wind, like rain.
He touched the trees, the beast, the man,
And whispered: "Live while still you can."

The World Begins Again

And mortals, hearing from afar,
Looked up again to moon and star.
They did not know from whence it came,
But something deep had changed the game.

They felt their lives not as a race,
But sacred moments wrapped in grace.
They laughed more deep, they held more near,
They sang not just from joy, but fear.

For now they knew what Time had shown,
That Life is sweet, but not alone.
That Death is not the end of song,
But simply where new notes belong.

And somewhere in the sky above,
Two shadows met, both dark and love.
They kissed again, no need to speak.

The world was strong. The world was weak.

But Time would keep it, all the same,
And every life would chant his name.

Coda: The Watcher Between Moments

Spoken in the voice of Time

I am Time, the ever-walk.
I do not sleep. I do not balk.
I stride between the stars and sand,
I hold the now in either hand.

You chase me, name me, break and bind,
But none escape me, none rewind.
You build your clocks and pray for more,
Yet never ask what came before.

Let me tell you, while I stay,
I am the child of Night and Day.
My mother laughs in bursting seeds,
My father waits where silence feeds.

I saw them once, in fire's birth,

Their union sparked the dust of Earth.
They made me not to rule or reign,
But to walk beside your joy and pain.

The Cycle Eternal

Each birth you hold within your arms
Is lit by Life's enduring charms.
Each ending, though it breaks your breath,
Is merely held by gentle Death.

I count them all. I watch, I keep.
The harvest and the dreamless sleep.
You think me cruel for how I flee,
But running is my destiny.

I'm not the tyrant you believe.
I do not take, I only weave.
Your stories, scars, your hopes, your fall,
I turn them into memory's hall.

A Whisper for the Living

So live. And let each heartbeat ring

As if you'll never see the spring.
But do not fear the final door,
My father's arms have held before.

And if you love, then love so vast
That Life herself will breathe it last.
And when you laugh, laugh loud and true,
The stars remember all you do.

For you are born of kiss and flame,
Of endless dark and endless name.
A mortal spark, yet still divine,
You walk with Death, with Life, with Time.

Thus ends the tale of First and Last,
Of Love that blooms, and Love that passed.
But every hour you rise anew,
Their ancient story lives in you.

www.ingramcontent.com/pod-product-compliance
Lightning Source LLC
Chambersburg PA
CBHW040245010526
44119CB00057B/824